If You Beat the Voice, You Beat the Enemy

By

Jason Thomas

Gotham Books

30 N Gould St.
Ste. 20820, Sheridan, WY 82801
https://gothambooksinc.com/

Phone: 1 (307) 464-7800

© 2023 *Jason Thomas*. All rights reserved.

No part of this book may be reproduced, stored in a retrieval system, or transmitted by any means without the written permission of the author.

Published by Gotham Books (May 19, 2023)

ISBN: 979-8-88775-283-9 (P)
ISBN: 979-8-88775-284-6 (E)

Because of the dynamic nature of the Internet, any web addresses or links contained in this book may have changed since publication and may no longer be valid.

The views expressed in this work are solely those of the author and do not necessarily reflect the views of the publisher, and the publisher hereby disclaims any responsibility for them.

Dedication Page

This book is dedicated to my beloved children, to my brothers and sisters in Christ. Also, to all the human race.

Preface

Everybody is talking. Everyone has something to say, even if they are not physically speaking. Everybody and everything are displaying a message one way or another. No matter how it comes or where it comes from, a voice is being heard. A message is getting across to someone by "somebody" and received by somebody. No matter what color, race, or gender you are, you are giving and receiving a message. My point of view on writing this book is to help people see that it's only two voices in this world and we can only choose one. Whose report are you going to believe? (Isaiah 53:1) You might be saying to yourself, "Well what are the two voices in the world?" Well, I am glad you asked, the two voices are God and Satan. These two are the only voices you can choose in life. One speaks life and one speaks death. In this world, in this life, you are only dying to live or living to die but you can't choose both, only one. My focus is to enlighten you on who is talking and how you distinguish between the two. Our life and world are created, fulfilled, and completed by words. Words are one of the most important things in life itself. I also want to reveal and understand who is speaking them and where they are leading you to. What type of picture is it painting in my imagination? Why are these thoughts coming to my mind? How and where do they come from? I've never thought about anything like that. These are some questions we may have asked ourselves, not knowing where they come from or where they are leading us to. This can be a big problem for humanity. It's easy to be deceived and lead down a path of defeat and death.

Table of Contents

Dedication

Preface

Introduction

Chapter 1	Voices	1
	Food For Thought	3
Chapter 2	Words are Power	5
Chapter 3	Where Did That Come From	9
	Note To Stay Focus	11
Chapter 4	Whose Report are You Going to Believe?	13
	Food for Thought	16
Chapter 5	Facts, Truth and Lies	17
	(The Foundation)	17
Chapter 6	Facts, Truth, and Lies (Pt.2 The Breakdown)	21
Chapter 7	Satan Is Only A Voice Going Against the Truth	27
Chapter 8	How You Beat the Voice	31
Chapter 9	Beating the Voice (breakdown)	35
Chapter 10	Limitations	39
Chapter 11	From Experience	41
Author Biography		45

Chapter 1

Voices

Voice, something we hear all the time. But what is it exactly? It is the sound produced in a person's larynx and uttered through the mouth, as a speech or song. It's also a particular opinion or attitude expressed by something or someone. Most of all it's words expressed through someone of their choice of thought and opinion. But understanding voice and how it operates, it's still a level of voice we miss that is not produced by a human being. It is not generated by one's larynx or uttered through one's mouth to produce speech (physically that is what we call in the natural). In the natural meaning, it is something tangible, something you can touch or see with your natural eyes (meaning 5 senses). As one having a physical conversation with someone else, and it's clear they are talking and expressing their thoughts and opinions to you. That is the level of voice we are adapted to. Or, even the voice of one that is in our memory, as a level of conscience remembering what parents or grandparents expressed to us out of their thought and opinion. But even that voice has a memory or origin of where it comes from. What about a level of voice that speaks through the eyes from the retina into a thought? I'm talking about words being spoken from something you see as a picture, that is not naturally or physically being spoken to you directly, but indirectly, it still speaks. When you look at something, all thoughts start to generate and speak. Looking at something gives substance to the retina and the mind starts to reason. Thoughts start to form based on the understanding of how one's preparation is programmed. For instance, that is why I can pour water in a glass cup halfway and get two different perceptions from the picture. It's halfway full or halfway empty. Even that level of voice has something to reason with, as comprehended that it was created or produced by someone, likely a human being. As long as the mind has something to reason with, the voice of that which speaks is still a voice that is predicted as the normal. The voice that I'm writing about is a level of voice that we fail to understand and comprehend. It is a voice that has no picture, no substance, nothing that's tangible to give it an origin and platform to penpoint who or where it's coming from. This voice is hard to distinguish. If one does not (know) or have a personal relationship to understand its character and direction of influence. This voice is not loud or forceful, it's subtle and gentle. This voice is a thought or expression that comes out of nowhere. Sometimes we reason with it and think it comes from us because our mind gives sound to it to be able to hear it within ourselves but, not knowing due to the lack of an intimate relationship with God, our father and creator of all, we tend to get tricked and deceived by the voice of our enemy, which is Satan. Satan can imitate anyone's voice to get our attention to try to infiltrate the mind to gain access to the body. His main weapon is deception. To deceive one mentally, to change the perception of something, and to make the truth look like a lie. Understand the voice who is speaking, see where it comes from, what its meaning and purpose is, and where the voice is trying to take you.

Food For Thought

We all are subject to different voices; I believe it's safe to say that we all can agree to being challenged by different voices in the world. We as human beings are raised and guided by voices in our life. For example…I remember when I was young a little boy about the age of 5 years old, my momma would allow me to play in the front yard, as I explored the wonders of mother nature, I would venture off headed towards the street not really knowing that I'm going into Danger Zone! My mom would say, "Hey come back in this yard, don't go in that street!" You can get hit by a car! Now from then on even if she wasn't there, her voice would replay my head every time & get close to the street, "Don't go in that street, you can get hit by a car!" Now this where it gets challenging…Due to the fact that my mom just stepped in the house for a quick second, so she's not physically sitting there watching Me. A voice pops up in my head and challenges my moms' words. And says, "Go into the street you're a big boy, it's going to be ok, you're not going to get hurt!" Boom! Now where did that voice come from, I have no one else here with me, I'm playing by myself, but something or someone is trying to get me to go against the one who truly loves and cares about me!???

Chapter 2

Words are Power

I know we talked about the voice and how significant it is, but what makes it so important? What is the essence of a voice? Is it the sound? A certain pitch or tone? Or maybe it's just the way it's said. That could be true in some cases, but a voice is only relevant and powerful because of (words). Without words, a voice is irrelevant. It has no substance, purpose, or nothing of essence. Words are the essence of a voice and they are powerful. They create, build up, tear down, and most of all they make everything if life manifest. Words are the substance to one's belief, as the Bible says: (Luke 6:45) "Out of the abundance of the heart the mouth speaks". The abundance in the heart is what you believe the most, it's what you have confidence and trust in. Sometimes without consciously thinking about what you believe, it comes out of ignorance through your voice, due to certain situations that challenges your belief system, your expectations, and one's perception. Words are powerful! Actually, they are so powerful that God created this world and all that is in it by speaking it into existence. (Genesis 1:1-28). God is God all by himself. He is truth, confidence, and power alone. So, when he speaks by faith, everything he speaks comes to pass due to his words and the understanding and wisdom he has of knowing the power of words. God also made us as human beings in his image, in his likeness, to do as he did, speak, create, build up, form and manifest with our words. In (Proverbs 18:21) it says, death and life are in the power of the tongue. Think about that for a minute. Death is the end of existing, and life is the beginning of existence. To meditate and understand that is to know the power of words. If death and life is in the power of our words we speak, that is meaning everything in between (life and death) is manifested through our words. If we can bring things to existence that were not existent before, and stop things that were existing to nonexistent, that means with our words, we have the power to make anything we think, speak, and believe manifest in this world. Knowing that, it is very important that we choose our words carefully. Knowing that every word we speak, once it's released from the heart through the larynx into the atmosphere, which means the spiritual realm, the realm we can't see. Like the air that blows, but none knows where or what direction it comes from. It can be felt or heard at times, but by faith we know it's there. Our words are spirit, meaning breath or wind. You hear them and sometimes they are felt when they are released. They affect our emotions and are powerful enough to cause an action… words are real!

You cannot see them physically, but the cause and effect of the aftermath of words being released, we see day by day. Most things in life are caused by words, no matter if they were verbally spoken or spoken in the battlefield of the mind. Words are the origin of the action caused by the effect it had on one's belief system. Words may, or may not inspire, they can build up or tear down, they can motivate or be unmotivated, and they can cause a positive or negative action. Thus, for future reference, think about your thinking, guard your mouth, do not let anything that you don't desire come out of your mouth.

Chapter 3

Where Did That Come From

Now that we have some type of understanding about how powerful words are and how effective they are in life… words are still creating, they are still building, they are still the substance behind cause and effect throughout life. They are the beginning and end of things, in both the spiritual and physical realm, they play a part in both atmospheres. Knowing this is essential, but it's only a part of the revelation I am unveiling to you. Even in knowing how powerful words are and how vital they may be, if one does not know where they come from or the origin of its existence, we still fail at knowing what or who to believe in. A lot of ideas and thoughts pass through our minds on a regular basis. Some of them are based on our perception of life due to issues and situations we may have been through in our lifetime. Thoughts are formed in many ways, but its origin is only from two sources, God and Satan, good and evil, light and darkness. I know some may say, "What about my thoughts? What about the things that "I" come up with in my own mind, reasoning with my own perception?" Yes, you are absolutely right. One does have the power to control thought and shape, his or her thought process. But no matter what you've thought about or what thoughts have popped up in your head, that you had no control over, its origin is still from the essence of God and Satan. These two entities, or shall I say powers, in the world are the only two voices in some kind of way connected to our words and perception of life. This whole world, this battle that we have in the mind, spiritual and physical sense, all revolves around them (two). Whether we believe it or not! Everything is reasoned between positive and negative, right or wrong, good or bad. I think you get where I'm coming from, but before I close this chapter, I want you to know this truth about God and Satan. God is God all by himself. He is power over all power, and nothing can stop or defeat him. God is good and he is love. He is lord of all lords, king of all kings, and remember this He is (not) in a battle with Satan, Satan is already defeated. His power has been stripped and taken away. Satan is just a voice going against the truth. Sometimes it looks like he has all the power, but in reality, he doesn't. He is powerless, he can only deceive you to empower his thoughts and actions by tricking you into believing his words, "what he says". Once you give into Satan's word, which is his thoughts, then only by your actions, we give him power on earth. If no one on earth would yield to Satan's thoughts, we would never see evil on earth. Satan can't "make" anyone do anything they don't want to do. Everything in life we do or don't, is by choice. Nothing is forced. We as human beings on earth have the power of choice. God gave us authority on earth. Due to our fleshly bodies being born here, it gives us citizenship authority on earth. Nothing on this earth is performed without our involvement. We give substance to spiritual words and thoughts to manifest on earth. It has to come through us. God created heaven and earth for us. We lost our authority due to Adam and Eve submitting to the lies and trickery of Satan about the fruit on the tree, and caused us to act against God's word, and still today is the same battle. Of whose report are you going to believe?

A NOTE TO STAY FOCUSED

Now remember this book is written to help us beat the voices in our head, to help you overcome the defeat, and the battles in your mind. We are all winners, we are all great, but some, like myself, didn't understand the fight of life. This means the character or person you desire to be, but can't achieve, that person and settling for whatever life throws at us. So, stay focused. I pray the rest of this book gives you the understanding and knowledge you need to unlock the power you have within us to live life. As an overcomer in all areas of life, remember the game of life is first won mentally, and it manifests physically.

Chapter 4

Whose Report are You Going to Believe?

This title is based on a scripture in the bible, Isaiah 53:1. Which the prophet Isiah had spoken about the coming of Jesus Christ and his purpose on earth for all mankind. I chose this title because it holds value to the understanding of the power of choice. This question is asked by God through Isaiah to us as people. Think about it, God created heaven and earth is giving us the freedom to choose. Choose what, one may ask? Choose to believe what God said or not. Some may say, "Oh I haven't made a choice yet" or "I don't believe in God", but either way we are still making a choice by not choosing. God is truth all by himself. He needs no one to believe him for his word to be true, but he wants us to believe him because it is the truth. Now that we've got that foundation established, I want you to remember that it's only two choices in the world. Indirectly, it seems like life is full of choices and unfortunately, it is. But its direction of many choices is leading you to only two directions, God or Satan. Knowing this allows making choices in life much simpler, knowing that each choice is leading you to only one way or another. For example, if you see something that doesn't belong to you and you pick it up, knowing who it's for, at that moment you have a choice to make. Give it back to the rightful owner or keep it for yourself. Now look into the scenario and understand the direction of choice one can make. Ask yourself which choice would fall behind God and which would fall behind Satan. Each decision you make in life is balanced by these two entities, no matter if it's far-fetched or right in hand. Know that your decisions in life are leading you in the direction of one or the other, mentally then physically. So, knowing the character and attributes of each one helps you choose based on the direction you desire to go in. Knowing where your choices are leading you allows you to become the owner of your destiny. Understanding the power of choice helps you to make better and wiser decisions. Knowing that your destiny lies in your own hand, through the decisions one makes through the course of life. Try meditating on that throughout the day. Now as our mind captivates and our spirit discerns the words of wisdom, I just shared with you, we have to gain an understanding on what was the plan from the beginning, from before the fall of man (Adam). Before the fall of Adam or before Adam disobeyed God, there was no sin. Everything God created was good and perfect. Man knew no wrong, no evil, no hate and because man knew nothing evil, man didn't think or speak evil. Evil couldn't be manifested in man's atmosphere because it wasn't known. If man doesn't think or speak it, it can't be manifested on earth. (Man is the portal and matrix of things. Being manifested from the spiritual realm to the natural realm that we can see). Understanding that statement is very important. It's saying that nothing can be established on earth unless man thinks or speaks it. (Remember there is power in the tongue of mankind). Now one may ask where does sickness and disease come from? Sickness and disease came from the fall as well. God commanded Adam and Eve not to eat from a certain tree, and if they did, they would die. Well Satan, which came as a serpent, deceived them into going against God's word. Because of that sin, the world now has a curse and we were separated from God and removed from the place of which we were in a perfect world called "Eden". A place where there was no sickness, no sin, no evil, and prosperity in abundance, no lack or want, absolutely perfect. One may be thinking, "well I had nothing to do with that", and you're right. Nevertheless, God made a way to reconcile us back to him, back in the garden of Eden, back into a relationship like it was in the beginning as one. That's the purpose of the gospel meaning too good to be true, or good news. God's message to us is so good, it's hard to believe with the natural mind, one must have the spirit of God to believe and accept the good news.

Food for Thought:

Remember when I shared with you all, about my mom telling me to not go into the street cause I can get hit by a car, then I was challenged with another voice that was going against my mother's command. Well, I was 5 years old, and I can remember, but age ain't nothing but number when it comes to making choices. I was 5 years old and was challenged (Who's report are you going to believe?) to make a choice on who's report I believed. Do I go with the one who I know loves me and cares for me, or do I go with this voice that's trying to boast my Ego and tell me I'm a Big Boy, I can do it, I won't get hit by a car, a voice I don't know where it comes from or who it is. At that moment, on the edge of the street, I have a choice to make, and no one in the world can make that choice for me. It's ME, the two voices and the knowledge and understanding I have of the decision I'm about to make. Thinking about thinking, causes me to question both choices and reason the outcome and origin of the two statements. To gain a clear understanding of who's report is in my best interest!

Chapter 5

Facts, Truth and Lies

(The Foundation)

This chapter out of all is the essence of the purpose of why I wrote this book. It's the root issue of the power of choice and the foundation of whose report are you going to believe. This chapter will clearly open your understanding to the battlefield of the mind, and how the power of choice is at your will. One's destiny is chosen by a multitude of choices one makes. Truth and lies is the makeup of our thought process and the heart of thinking. All mankind's thoughts are divided up into three things: fact, truth, and lies. Before I open up and challenge your thinking, I want to give you the layout of how life became the battle between these three choices. Before the fall of man when man disobeyed God, life wasn't made up of choices based on what's true or false. This battle came when man disobeyed God and ate from the tree of knowledge of knowing good and evil. Mankind didn't know evil at all before the fall. Everything God created was good. Therefore, if all we knew was good, then only good can shape our atmosphere. (Remember I told you nothing can manifest on this earth without us, everything has to come through us one way or another.) We are the vehicle that manifestation from the thought (spiritual) realm materializes on earth. Everything is materialized through us. Now Satan knew through us everything is manifested, but he also knew that he couldn't tempt us with evil because we knew no evil, only good. Consequently, his mission was to deceive us into eating from the tree of knowledge of knowing good and evil. Now since we know evil, we can be tempted in our thought process to choose and act on evil. This is when the power of choice got complicated. Due to the fact that evil is present in our thought process, now it's a challenge to choose good thoughts that are warring against evil thoughts. Truth is still truth all by itself, but now lies can dictate and infiltrate the truth, causing the birth and power of facts. Fact is a tool that helps us make a choice between two decisions. It's also a thing that is known, or proved to be true. Before evil came into the process of thought, truth was truth, and didn't need fact to prove that truth is not a lie. Now in our present state of life, we are use to warring with what is truth and what is a lie. This is the foundation of the battlefield of the mind. This is the source of cause and effect in our lives. This is the essence of faith, the choice to believe what God said is truth. Now let's look at truth. Truth is from God, anything he says is truth. But when the power of choice and free will is in the midst, one's faith can believe otherwise and cause the other voice to be true in one's life. (Remember it's only two voices in the world, God or Satan) so if one is not believing in what God said to be his truth, then the only other word he can believe in is the lies of Satan. And because one has the power of choice and free will he chooses to believe in Satan's lies and causes it to be true in his life. Now that doesn't make God's word to be a lie because God's word is the truth alone. Even if one doesn't believe in it, it's true just because God said it. Now, since the fall of mankind, mankind has been confused on what is the truth and what is a lie. But by the grace of God, God even uses the tool of fact, not to prove that his word is true, but to prove to us that truth is his word. God only uses the tool of fact to convince us that Satan is a liar and to help mankind distinguish between what's truth and what's not. God loves us so much that he doesn't want his children to be deceived by the enemy, he wants us to know who we really are, and do all that he planned for us to do and be. God wants us to live like how it was in the beginning, in the garden of Eden before the fall, when everything was good. He desires for us to live in abundance, in good health, in peace and true joy, not in lack, fear or danger, but in prosperity in holiness, one with him again.

Chapter 6

Facts, Truth, and Lies

(Pt.2 The Breakdown)

Now that we got the foundation out of the way on how fact and lies came in the midst of truth, I want to challenge your thinking on a few scenarios that wars with our decision making to discern what is truth and what's not. We all as people, no matter the color, background or race, no matter the IQ level, gender, or age, are familiar with the battlefield of the mind. The battle to believe what is truth or what is a lie, to discern what is good and what's evil, to distinguish if this is from God or Satan. We all have struggled with the power of freewill to choose to believe what we believe, that may be truth in any situation. We all have had this mental battle in some form or fashion. No matter if it's a situation where something is not yours, you're struggling mentally whether to take it or not, or something as common as you warring with yourself of who you are or how you perceive yourself to be, which is now called a form of depression. No matter the issue at hand, we all have battled in our minds one way or another. My goal for writing this book is to help one beat the battle mentally before it manifests physically, or to help one beat the battle mentally to change the physical appearance. Sometimes in life due to the fall of mankind, life deals us a hand that's complicated and sometimes hard to cope with. Because of our lack of understanding life itself and who we really are as human beings and how this whole thing works called life. It tends to overwhelm us in our mental state of mind, by walking in what we call darkness, ignorance, or even enigmatic life. That's a life that is full of mysteries, a life of the unknown, not sure of what to make out of it. Kind of like "wherever the wind blows that's the way we go". But I'm here to tell you that it's a certainty of life. It's a true understanding and a confidence about life that we as humans can be in control of our outcome of choice and the masters of our fate. Destiny can be controlled by faith, the belief and one's confidence of knowing the end from the beginning, and the ability to focus on just that. With a true understanding of the power and authority of mankind on earth (life gets understandable) to the point where peace resides in our mind and hearts, knowing that everything is okay and under control by the power of choice. I say all that to let you know that you don't have to settle for the pop ups in your life or the outcome that life tries to choose for you. Remember "God said he created us in his image to have dominion over all the earth (Gen. 1:26-29)" and every living thing that moves on the earth. Catch that for a moment (every living thing)... Anything that moves, anything that grows, anything that manifests itself on earth, we as human beings have dominion over it. Dominion is sovereignty or control of a territory, so anything that materializes in our territory we are in control of. The earth is our territory, God said to have dominion over all the earth. God gave us the ability and authority to rule and govern the whole earth. For example, cancer is a disease that forms in human beings' cell system. We can't see it but we can detect it, and by doing so we know that cancer is present in the body. Knowing that we have to remember God said that we have dominion over all things that creeps on earth, so if it manifests itself on earth, it's under our dominion. We have control over it, with the belief of what God said. Now you may ask, "why do people die from it if we have control over it?" Good question! I'm glad you asked, lack of knowledge! The lack of knowledge and understanding of who we are and the authority God gave us and our position on earth as a human being is what causes us to be defeated by anything that's not of God. (Hosea 4:6) says, "My people are destroyed for lack of knowledge, meaning the mystery of the power and authority of man-kind. Our authority to rule on earth keeps us in a defeated lifestyle, not knowing causes us to allow things to have victory in our lives." I'm sure most of us have heard this statement before, but because of the norm and what we see in life most of the time dictates our perception to see things as

God said them. This is the fight of faith, fighting mentally to believe what God said or to believe what is at hand in the present moment, of which is the proven fact to be true at the present time. Now I'm not saying cancer didn't grow in your body, or you don't have the symptoms they have proven as a (fact) to be true. What I'm saying is yes. It's a fact, proven evidence by tests and an outward appearance that what you are experiencing is present at the moment, and looks like your truth. I'm here to shake you up and tell you that it is fact, but it doesn't have to be your truth just because it's proven to be factual. You have the authority to believe and call those things that's not, to be true in your life. Yes, I've been diagnosed with a disease or sickness, but God said I'm healed. This is where the battle starts, fact vs. truth. Whose report are you going to believe? Remember the title of this book is called ("If you beat the voice, you beat the enemy." The enemy is creating thoughts, issues, and scenarios, mentally and physically. And we as people of God are allowing it to be truth in our life, by excepting anything that's not from God. (if it don't come from God, by all means it is to not be excepted). All things from God are good, in the beginning everything God made and created was good. Nothing bad existed. Remember receiving Christ in our hearts takes away the power of sin, and brings us back to the beginning in the peace and abundance of the garden of Eden. The garden of Eden is a mindset, it's a destiny of one's belief system. If you believe it, you can experience Eden on earth now. Like I said it can be a proven fact you are sick but God said you are healed. It's a proven fact by your bank account that you are broke but God said you are rich, by his riches and glory in Jesus Christ. (Whose report are you going to believe?) That's where the fight of faith begins, when there are two choices but only one decision can be purposefully chosen. Without knowing God and a revelation of who we are in Christ, "my people will perish for the lack of knowledge". We perish or overtaken by something that's supposed to be under our authority due to the fact of not knowing… and not knowing comes from not having a relationship with the one who created everything. Having a relationship with God allows you to understand self and capabilities one already possesses within. I can testify all day about the authority and capabilities God said we, as people, have or the things I've experienced and seen God make to come to pass that validates his word to be true. But, if I can be honest with you, that will not do anything. It takes one to seek and search individuality and allow God to reveal the revelation of who they are in Christ as one with God. This walk of faith is personal, but it's for every human being who is willing to labor to seek out the mysteries of life, to live as an overcomer. One who wins in every situation. Now as I close this chapter, I want you to remember that all things are possible with God, only with God. I'm not saying it's easy, but it's possible and if it's possible then with the power of God, God will see you through. Sometimes it may look like it's not working with your physical eyes, but faith is the substance of things hoped for and evidence of things not seen. So don't go off of what it looks or feels like, just stand on what God said. Keep saying the truth until it changes the fact, then the truth which is God's word will prove to be true in your life and that's a proven fact.

Chapter 7

Satan Is Only A Voice Going Against the Truth

The understanding of this statement is the essence of winning the battle in the mind. Knowing this truth about our adversary gives us the upper hand and ability to overcome Satan and his lies. His goal is to kill, steal, and destroy (John 10:10). He's trying to kill your hope, hope is the beginning of faith, faith is the vehicle to manifest the promises of God from the spiritual to physical realm. It's how you believe and achieve what you need pertaining to life. He comes to steal all that you've got, mostly your time and attention. If he can keep you distracted, not knowing who you are and what you already possess, then he knows he can continuously keep you in a defeated lifestyle (because of the lack of knowledge). It's not that people don't want you to win, but if you don't know something, you can't do anything. Last but not least he comes to destroy. Destroy means to put an end to the existence of something by damaging or attacking it. Satan is trying to take us out, he is trying to kill our existence on earth, and cause us not to know God and who we are; to be eternally separated from God forever by keeping us distracted from

God's salvation plan into a victorious and perfect will. His goal is to keep us in the unknown, to keep us ignorant to what is really at hand, and that is he is defeated. Yes, Satan is defeated. He has no power, no authority in your life. He is only a voice going against the truth. (He is all talk). One may ask, "How is he the cause of so much turmoil if he is defeated?" Good question... because we give him authority in our lives to cause so much turmoil, by not knowing our enemy. Not knowing who we are and the authority we possess. I'm going to enlighten you on our adversary and how I know he has no power. For one, (Colossian 2:14-15) says that Christ disarmed principalities & powers, then in (Luke 4:1-13), it shows that he can only try to convince you into submitting to his lies. Physically, he can't harm us but he can deceive us into harming ourselves. Deceive meaning to cause someone to believe something that is not true, typically in order to gain some personal advantage. Think about that for a moment... our adversary number one tool is to deceive or trick one into believing a lie, something that is not true. On the other hand, his goal is to make you think that a lie is truth to gain an advantage, an advantage of what one may ask? The control of thought and the position of one's ability to imagine. I once heard a wise man say, "if you control the mind, you control the whole body". Therefore, if our adversary is trying to deceive us into believing a lie is truth, then that tells me he is trying to gain control of my mind to dictate my thoughts and take advantage of the power of choice in what I believe is truth. If our adversary takes control of our thoughts, he then has control of our imagination. Our imagination is the matrix process to cause something to manifest. It's where your belief, the things that you've decided to be your truth and vision. It's how you see and imagine things to be based on what you believe comes together which is called faith, and causes it to manifest in the physical world. With the understanding of that, you can see why our adversary is after our minds. With the control of one's mind, you control their beliefs and their actions. By controlling one's actions, you basically control them. By controlling them, he controls your life which controls your destiny. This is the plan and fight that the enemy is trying to cause in all our lives. The only way he has power on earth is if he tricks us into giving it to him. If he can gain your choice of thought, then he dictates what is true or not in your life. We have to learn what truth is and then we will know what is a lie. To fight the fight of faith, to take hold of only what God said is true, not what the enemy is creating to look like truth. So, once you know truth, stand on it. No matter what it feels or looks like, God will do what he said. Now remember (the adversary is only a voice going against the truth.)

Chapter 8

How You Beat the Voice

Knowing that our adversary is a voice going against the truth, we now understand that truth is the key to overcoming the enemy. I want to start this chapter off by saying, you can't defeat the enemy alone. Our words, our thoughts, our strength, even our intelligence cannot overcome the adversary alone. It will take the help of God's spirit and power to detect and overcome the enemy's plots and schemes. Always remember God said in the beginning that he is craftier than any beast on earth, so never think that without God you can win. Even if it looks or feels like you're winning, just know you're not. It's what he wants you to think. It's deception. The reason why I say this is because God has the truth about who you are, and what you possess as a human being. That's facts that can't be altered unless one chooses not to believe in the truth that God spoke of oneself. The essence of using God's truth is because God's truth is the origin about you before the fall or before sin came into existence. "What truth is that?" one may ask. That truth is simple, that everything is good. See, when God made everything in the beginning, he said everything was good. Now that Christ came and paid for sin, we are back in the beginning, in the garden of Eden, where everything is very good. Now you may have some challenges to believe the goodness of God like in the garden of Eden could be possible, now in this day in age, due to all the turmoil we see in the earth. But it's possible. He never said it was easy, but he said all things are possible with God. I use God's truth because his truth in every situation is good. His truth comes from a pure heart of love, and his truth always works in our favor. But we have the will, power, and freedom to believe what we choose to believe. Some may believe in what the coach told us when we were young or what our parents kept repeating to us out of ignorance of knowing who we are or can be. Some believe the doctor that says you've only got two weeks to live, or the teacher that says you'll never be anything. We have the power to choose where our origin of truth comes from. The truth of the matter is, whose report are you going to believe? We have to remember everything and everybody is speaking in some form or fashion, and everything in some type of way is trying to shape our perception based on how they see it. Everything changes in the world, so our perception in one situation may be different in another, due to the issue at hand. But God's truth and perception never changes. His word is law no matter what. Remember he is the creator who creates, so in any situation he can make or cause his word to be true. So when the enemy comes with a bad report or those negative thoughts about you are not worthy, you can't do it, don't nobody love you or they diagnose you based on the nature of the problem by examination of the symptoms and say you have this or you are this type of person. With the truth of God, you can counteract the lies of the enemy. When the enemy says you can't do it, God says you can do all things, when the enemy says you are not worthy, you say what God said about you. You are fearfully and wonderfully made out of love. When they diagnose you with a disease you can stand on (Psalm 103:2-3) forget not all these benefits… who heals all your diseases. Now as you can see the battle to believe is based on words, whose report are you going to believe? Now the difference between the voice of God and the voice of the world is the world is speaking from perception formed from experience throughout life and God is speaking from truth being the creator who creates everything. Most importantly I want you to remember that the truth God speaks, he doesn't expect you to cause it to come to pass, he causes it to come true in your life by himself. The only obligation you have is to believe. Everything that God speaks is truth so anything that speaks differently is a voice going against the truth. You as an individual have to rebuke the voice of the world, and hold on to the voice of God, but in order to do that you have to know what God said about that situation. Once you know what God said about that situation you hold on to it. You speak it until you gain confidence that it will be truth in your life. God's word will never come back void.

Chapter 9

Beating the Voice (breakdown)

Now that we've gone over "how to beat the voice", I wanted to close it out with a breakdown to clearly convey the steps and process of overcoming the voice. First, speaking on something multiple times is needed, it's called repetition. Repeating something is a form of meditation. Meditation is the essence of getting it into the subconscious to remember it when needed. Now remember that the fight is with words, the battle is within your mind. Whoever gets control of the mind automatically gains control of the body. Now the simplicity of beating the voice is easy, meditate on these pointers: "Always think about your thinking." When thoughts come to mind you have to take hold of them and challenge it. Ask yourself where did this resonate from, who is the source? Is it in line with the truth of what God said about you or whatever situation is at hand? That's why in God's word it says, "take every thought captive..." and that means every thought. It's important and possible to do. God knows that our mind has to be governed and watched over because it's the control center of our thoughts and manifestations on earth. The mind is the matrix of the filling of earth. Everything you see now with your eyes comes from someone's mind. Just knowing that you can see that the mind is very important. Thus, God teaches us to protect it by all means after you take hold of your thought and examine it. Once you detect that it's not lined up with the truth, then you cast it out by simply rebuking it or just saying, "I do not accept that in my life", then replace it with what you desire in your life. "Food for thought" that's why it's important to know the truth about oneself and the truth in any situation in life because when negative and challenging thoughts come, you have to have something to replace it with. The thought has to be truth, something you believe and have confidence in, about the thought that's challenging you. Everything is a fight mentally with words. Words are a weapon, or tool, everyone uses to overcome or be defeated. We lack understanding how important words are, words created the earth, filled the earth, and is governed by the earth and everything in it. Words that were spoken by the enemy that we believed in, caused sickness and disease to come into the earth. Now if we can believe in the wrong words and it produced an action that caused us to be in turmoil, defeat, sickness, poverty, lack, anxiety, depression, and much more that wasn't meant, then we sure can believe in the right words which are true. This causes the opposite to manifest which is healing, abundance, prosperity, joy, peace, and much more that was meant for us before the deception of the enemy. Never just believe that all you go through and all you see is all that life has to offer. It's much more to life than we can phantom. The mind has the ability to manifest anything that your spirit and soul can believe. So do not fear, beat the enemy by beating the voice that's going against the truth!

Chapter 10

Limitations

LIMITATIONS To sum this whole thing up "if you beat the voice, you beat the enemy" our biggest enemy is ourself! No matter who said what, or what the adversary which is the enemy is doing to cause us not to become who we are destined to be. In Spite of all the distractions that's meant to cause us to not achieve our greatest ability, it's still our own thinking that limits us on our ability to do anything we set our mind to achieve. No matter what we have heard, seen or experienced it's on each individual to choose what they except to believe to be their truth. Your limitations are controlled by your beliefs, whatever a person believes sets his or her boundaries to be limited to how far they can go. One cannot, "I repeat" one cannot go further than what they believe. You may have a vision of something great, but if you don't believe you can achieve that vision of greatness, you'll never experience that goal or vision come to pass in your life. It's our job to clean our mind out of all the negative and discouraging words that we have accumulated over time. Our mind is a garden and we are the gardeners of our mind. No one can tend to your garden but you we have the job of pulling out weeds that's not supposed to be there, we have to fertilize, prune and whatever else it takes to keep your mind (garden) healthy and blooming. That's why it's important to know your truth about who you really are and what you possess as a human being. Without knowing the truth of your ability, allows us to accept and believe things that we wouldn't accept if we knew our worth and value. Last thing I want you all to remember: ("Your attitude determines your altitude." Meaning it's how you think about things (perception) that dictates how far we go in life! It's all on you! You have the power of choice! Choose your destiny wisely.

Chapter 11

From Experience

Last but not the lease, I want to paint a clear picture for you all to see what it looks like to "beat the voice, you beat the enemy! From a personal experience and true situations in my life on how I overcame the voice of limitations in my head that was holding me back from elevating to my highest potential. Growing up as a kid I was raised in a poverty area that's called. The projects or hood. It was a world that's surrounded by crime, drugs gangs and violence. In such a place you can see the attributes of poverty, living in lack and in need it breeds disobedience, envy, jealousy and many more traits of evil... seeing this everyday caused me to adopt an image & vision of myself and how far I can go in life based on the things that surrounded me day by day as a kid. As l grew up eventually became a product of my environment, believing that this was my life and that's all it was out there for people of poverty." for a moment that was my truth, it was a fact to me because I adopted the image that limited me to only what I seen and was raised around, until later in life l found the truth! My highest potential of myself was being one of the biggest drug dealers from my neighborhood I thought that was the goal for my life at that time, tricked by the enemy.

Blinded by my surroundings, I was limited on who I was as a man and the power one possesses to become anything he puts his mind to. On my journey into thinking I would become the biggest drug dealer in my neighborhood, living a lie, tricked by the enemy. I end up going to prison a few times due to the life style I was living, and believing the lie I had adopted to be my truth. To make a long story short while I was in prison away from all the distractions and worldly influences that kept me from actually thinking about my thinking and my choices, I've made in my life that caused me to end up in, a place called prison. I realized that I was living a life of insanity.

That's doing the same thing over and over and expecting different results. That made me start thinking deeper into who I was, what I was doing and where my life was headed not to long after that I found the Lord Jesus Christ and in the process of learning and growing, I was challenged mentally by the Bible to change my thinking on how I viewed myself. As I read the bible it started to cause me to believe I was more than I thought I was or can be. It compelled me to believe I was greater than what my up bringing showed me. I started to change my vision about myself and started visualizing myself above and beyond the man I believed myself into. Now it wasn't easy but, simple. You'll still have those thoughts of who you use to be or who people say you were. It's what they called battlefield of the mind!" You're battling what your circumstances shaped you into vs. the truth of the power one possesses to become whatever one puts their mind to. This truth wasn't a factor at all to me when I was growing up but became a common denominator in my life to help me succeed to the man I am now.

It was a fight to believe and stand on what God said about my life verses what I been through and what I see on a daily basis. From me believing that I don't have what it takes to become more than a drug dealer, to God saying I have everything within me to become whatever I put my mind to. From me believing I'm not enough to God saying I'm more than enough, from me thinking I'll never win at life. To God saying am already victorious, in Him I already won.

The limitations I had of myself came from my circumstances and surroundings that birth in me the way I viewed myself. I learned that you can't surpass what you believed, and what you believe is what you become. Not being exposed to something greater than your perception will only allow you to go as far as what you believe. "The secret to life is vision," if you can see it, you can achieve it. But the flip side to that is... Even if your vision is positive or pessimistic, that which you believe you will receive. Now since I've adopted a new perception of myself, I see myself not as life shaped me to be, but as the truth that I discovered about who I truly was as a man. That's who I started to conform to. That's a man of "integrity, honor, ambition and most of all purpose". With the change of a mindset, I changed the fact of how I was shaped by my surroundings, to the truth of who I really was & that's greatness! I had to find truth about myself, to beat the voice of fact and limitations that I adopted due to my surroundings. Once I beat the Voice, I beat the enemy!

Author Biography

"If you beat the Voice, You beat the Enemy" was written by Jason Thomas an author that was born and raised in Beaumont, Texas and reared by his Grandmother due to drugs taking over his immediate family, which is his mother, two brothers and his sister. Jason grew up without a father figure in the house hold surrounded by drugs, crime and poverty. The odds were stacked against him from a child to at life, which he made many mistakes that lead him down a path to prison. While incarcerated Jason accepted Jesus Christ as his Lord and Savior, then begin to learn about God and who he was as a man. Jason begins to overcome his own beliefs and started to elevate into the person God destines for him to be. Upon release from prison after a decade, Jason was ready to achieve all that life has for him. It wasn't easy for Jason, but all things are possible with God. Challenges was present while on this new journey of success and righteousness, but Jason endured the test. While doing so, he has accomplished many things: His own trucking company, designer shoe line, created his own invention, wrote a book and launched his own Perfume Line. He also spreads the word of God to men who are incarcerated, giving them hope and building their faith to believe they can be greater than the world expects them to be.

www.ingramcontent.com/pod-product-compliance
Lightning Source LLC
LaVergne TN
LVHW052005060526
838201LV00059B/3842